Hedgehog

A Fun and Educational Book for Kids with Amazing Facts and Pictures

Table of Contents

Introduction

Little, insectivorous animals known as hedgehogs are widespread throughout much of Europe, Asia, and Africa. There are around 17 different types of hedgehogs, but the European hedgehog is the most prevalent and well-known (Erinaceus europaeus).

Spines, which are actually repurposed hairs, cover hedgehogs. They defend themselves from predators by using their spines. They will curl into a ball when frightened, leaving only their spines exposed, making them challenging to attack.

Hedgehogs have additional adaptations that help them live in their natural surroundings in addition to their spines. They have weak vision, but a keen sense of smell and hearing that they employ to find prey and avoid danger. Hedgehogs are adept climbers and swimmers as well.

Hedgehogs are mainly nocturnal creatures that spend a lot of time searching for food. Together with other insects, they also consume small animals like mice and frogs. Fruits, berries, and other plant stuff are also reported to be eaten by them.

Hedgehogs are favored pets in many parts of the world, yet keeping them as pets is prohibited in several nations. They are threatened in the wild by habitat degradation, traffic, and canine and feline predators.

Hedgehog Name

Due to their environment and morphological characteristics, hedgehogs get their name. Hedgerows, which are rows of shrubs and trees sometimes used to divide fields and other land areas, are where hedgehogs are most commonly found. This connection to hedgerows is where the term "hedge" in "hedgehog" originates.

Hedgehogs have a habitat, as well as spines on their bodies that resemble the bristles on a hog or pig. This physical resemblance is where the word "hog" in hedgehog originates.

Hence, the term "hedgehog" refers to a pig-like creature that lives in hedgerows. The word has been in use at least since the 15th century and is still used to refer to these extraordinary and interesting animals.

Appearance

Hedgehogs are little mammals with rounded bodies and sharp spines all over them. Their body size varies from species to species, although the majority of species are between 15 and 30 cm (6 and 12 inches) long and weigh between 0.5 and 1.5 kg (1 to 3 pounds).

Hedgehogs' spines, which are formed of the hard protein keratin, are actually modified hairs. The hedgehog may curl into a tight ball and expose only its sharp, stiff spines when it feels frightened or scared, protecting itself from predators.

Hedgehogs feature beady eyes, short ears, and a pointed snout. Although they have weak vision, they have keen hearing and smell senses that help them locate prey and escape danger.

Hedgehog coloration varies depending on the species, although the majority have a dark underside and lighter-colored spines. While some species have more pronounced stripes or face patterns, others have a more uniform colouring.

Hedgehogs are popular pets and adored creatures in many cultures around the world because of their striking appearance.

Quills

Hedgehogs have spiky, prickly structures called quills that cover their sides and back. Contrary to common perception, these quills are really modified hairs composed of keratin, the same protein that makes up human hair and nails. They are not a component of the hedgehog's bones or body.

Thousands of quills cover the body of each hedgehog, acting as a barrier against predators. A hedgehog will roll into a tight ball with its quills jutting out in all directions when frightened or scared, forming a protective barrier that is challenging for predators to get through.

Hedgehogs have muscles that are connected to their quills on their back and sides, which gives them some control over their protective stance. The hedgehog can move its quills in reaction to cues like touch or temperature changes because to a small amount of muscular tissue at the base of each one.

Although a hedgehog's quills may appear sharp and menacing, they are not toxic or barbed, and they do not separate from the body of the hedgehog like a porcupine's do. Hedgehog quills can really be held safely and comfortably with correct handling because they are typically not dangerous to people.

Food

Hedgehogs are mostly insectivores, which means that their primary food source is insects and other tiny invertebrates. Beetles, caterpillars, and earthworms are a few of the most typical insects that hedgehogs consume. Hedgehogs have been observed to consume amphibians, birds, and small animals.

Hedgehogs eat fruit and berries as well as meat, making up the majority of their diet. Among other fruits, they have been observed to consume apples, pears, bananas, strawberries, and blackberries.

Due to their high metabolic rates, hedgehogs need a lot of food to stay energized. As a result, they are frequently opportunistic feeders, which means that they will consume any food that is offered to them in their natural environment.

A balanced diet is crucial for the health and wellbeing of pet hedgehogs. Commercial hedgehog food is readily available, but it's crucial to pick a top-notch brand that's made just for them. Hedgehogs kept as pets can be fed a variety of fresh fruits, vegetables, and cooked meats as part of a balanced diet in addition to commercial food. Foods heavy in sugar or fat should not be given to hedgehogs since these can have negative effects on their health.

Geography

Most of the world is home to hedgehogs, with the exception of Australia, Madagascar, and a few regions in North and South America, where they have not yet been introduced. Their most prevalent regions include Europe, Asia, and Africa.

Hedgehogs come in a variety of species, and each species has a unique geographic distribution. For instance, the long-eared hedgehog (Hemiechinus auritus) is found in portions of central Asia and the Middle East, whereas the European hedgehog (Erinaceus europaeus) may be found in most of Europe and western Asia. The Indian hedgehog (Paraechinus micropus) is found in India and some areas of Pakistan, but the desert hedgehog (Paraechinus aethiopicus) is located in North Africa and the Middle East.

Hedgehogs are aggressively managed or hunted in some locations because they are regarded as problem species. Hedgehogs are revered and safeguarded in many cultures, nevertheless, because of their function in regulating insect populations and as a sign of luck or fertility.

Senses

Hedgehogs possess a variety of senses that are vital to their ability to survive in the wild. Hedgehogs' most crucial senses include a few of the following:

Hedgehogs can detect danger and locate food using their excellent sense of smell. They mark their territory via scent glands on their foot and underside.

Hedgehogs can locate prey and identify predators thanks to their keen hearing. They have the ability to hear sounds that are audible only to animals.

Hedgehogs can feel vibrations and movements in their surroundings thanks to their sensitive whiskers. They locate prey by using their sense of touch to travel.

Taste: Hedgehogs have a keen sense of taste, which aids them in identifying and choosing healthy foods.

Hedgehogs are primarily active at night and rely on their other senses to travel and find food because they have weak eyesight.

In order to survive in the environment and maintain their health and well-being, hedgehogs rely extensively on their senses.

Habitat

Forests, grasslands, deserts, and suburban areas are just a few of the diverse habitats that hedgehogs can flourish in. Hedgerows, gardens, and parks are among the places where they can be found most frequently.

Hedgehogs generally build tunnels or nests out of grass, leaves, and other plants in the wild where they live. In addition, they can look for refuge under clumps of brush or leaves or inside the burrows of other animals.

Hedgehogs may settle in gardens, parks, and other green places in suburban and urban areas. They might also seek refuge behind decks, sheds, or other buildings.

Hedgehogs are generally resourceful and adaptable creatures that can live in a variety of locations as long as there is enough vegetation and cover to protect them.

Sounds

Although they tend to be silent animals, hedgehogs occasionally make noises to communicate or show emotion. Hedgehogs can generate a variety of sounds, including:

Hedgehogs may hiss to frighten off potential predators or other animals when they feel threatened or afraid. You can hear this sound by blowing through your teeth.

Snuffling: While a hedgehog is looking for food or examining its surroundings, it may snuffle or grunt.

Chirping: When hungry or in discomfort, baby hedgehogs, sometimes known as hoglets, may chirp or squeak.

Hedgehogs have been known to create a sound akin to a cat's purr when they are satisfied.

Hedgehogs have a reputation for snoring loudly while they are asleep.

Hedgehogs are generally not very vocal creatures, although they do occasionally make some noises to communicate and show emotion.

Mating

The Northern Hemisphere's average hedgehog breeding season, which lasts from May to September, is very brief. Male hedgehogs will actively look for females to mate with during this time.

A male hedgehog will often engage in a wooing dance when he discovers a female, which includes circling her and inhaling her scent. The female may arch her back and lift her quills to indicate that she is ready for a mate if she is receptive to his advances.

In hedgehogs, mating may be a noisy and occasionally violent process. During copulation, the male frequently bites the female on the neck or flanks. The female will depart on her own after mating in order to construct a nest and get ready to give birth to her offspring.

Hedgehogs are solitary creatures that don't establish enduring relationships with their partners. Males and females will part ways after the breeding season is over and live alone until the following breeding season.

Babies

Hedgehog hoglets, or baby hedgehogs, are born hairless, blind, and deaf. Hedgehogs typically have a 35-day gestation period, after which the female gives birth to a litter of one to seven hoglets.

The mother will milk the hoglets for around four to six weeks after birth, until they are weaned and able to eat solid food. The mother will remain near her nest during this period to safeguard and warm her young.

The hoglets will start to leave the nest and explore their surroundings once they have been weaned. Hedgehogs are born with a full set of quills, but they are initially pliable and fragile. As the hoglets grow, the quills get harder and sharper.

Around six months after birth, hedgehogs acquire sexual maturity and are then able to reproduce sexually and give birth to their own young. Most hedgehogs live between three and six years in the wild, which is a rather short lifespan for them.

Health

Hedgehogs, like all animals, are prone to a variety of health problems that may have an effect on how they feel. The following are a few of the most typical health conditions that hedgehogs may encounter:

Obesity: Overeating or inadequate exercise can cause hedgehogs to gain weight. Many health concerns, such as musculoskeletal and respiratory disorders, can be brought on by obesity.

Dental issues: Hedgehogs' teeth are always growing, so if they don't have enough to chew on, they may become overgrown and develop dental issues.

Hedgehogs are prone to skin conditions such dermatitis, fungal infections, and mites. Regular grooming and good hygiene can help prevent these problems.

Hedgehogs may get respiratory illnesses if they are maintained in filthy or moist conditions or are exposed to sick animals.

Fleas, ticks, and worms are just a few of the parasites that can infest hedgehogs. Preventative treatment and routine veterinarian exams can help stop parasite infestations.

To keep your hedgehog healthy and content, make sure they have access to a nutritious meal, a cozy living space, and frequent medical care. To avoid the problem getting worse, it's critical to get veterinarian attention as soon as you feel your hedgehog may be having any health problems.

Behavior

Hedgehogs are nocturnal creatures, which means that nighttime is when they are most active. They normally rest during the day in a nest or beneath a protected structure like a hedge, stump, or heap of leaves.

Hedgehogs are solitary creatures and are not typically gregarious creatures. They may form territories and protect them against competing hedgehogs, although they rarely interact outside of the breeding season.

Animals like hedgehogs move rather slowly; they frequently shuffle or walk on all fours. They can scale minor obstacles well and are strong climbers, although they lack the agility of other small animals like rats or squirrels.

Hedgehogs generally roll into a tight ball and expose their spiny quills as a form of defense when confronted. The act of "balling up" serves to dissuade predators from attacking them.

Due to their curiosity, hedgehogs may investigate their

surroundings by sniffing and prodding things with their snouts. They can find food and other resources using their keen sense of smell.

In general, hedgehogs are nocturnally active, solitary, and slow-moving creatures. They have a keen sense of smell, which they use to investigate their surroundings, and are well recognized for their defensive instinct of curling up into a tight ball when threatened.

Hibernation

It is well known that hedgehogs have the ability to hibernate, which is a profound sleep condition that enables them to store energy throughout the winter when food may be in short supply. As the temperature falls below a particular point, hedgehogs will often start to hibernate in the late fall or early winter.

The hedgehog slows down its metabolism and lowers its body temperature during hibernation to save energy. They may go for extended periods without eating or drinking, and their heart rate and respiration rate also slow down.

Before hibernating, hedgehogs usually make a nest, which can be found in a variety of locations, including under a log, in a pile of leaves, or in a burrow. While the hedgehog is hibernating, the nest provides insulation and protection from the weather.

During hibernation, hedgehogs may briefly awaken to walk around and adjust their position, but they normally go right back to sleep. The hedgehog will emerge from hibernation in the spring as the weather starts to warm up and resume its regular activities.

It's vital to understand that not all hedgehogs will hibernate; some may stay active all winter long if the weather stays moderate and there is food available. Hedgehogs who are young or ill might not be able to successfully hibernate and would need particular care to survive the winter.

Social life

Hedgehogs are mostly solitary creatures with weak social bonds. They are most active at night, when they hunt for food, investigate their surroundings, and construct nests. They frequently snooze during the day in a protected space, like a hedge, a pile of leaves, or a burrow.

Hedgehogs can set up territories and protect them from other hedgehogs, but they are not gregarious creatures and usually only interact with one another during the breeding season. The male hedgehog will abandon the female to raise the young alone after mating, which typically occurs in the late spring or early summer.

Although hedgehogs live alone, it's vital to remember that socializing with their human caregivers can still be beneficial to them. Spending time with your hedgehog, giving them enrichment opportunities, and providing a nice home are all things that can help to make sure they're content and healthy. In order to keep your hedgehog cognitively active and avoid boredom, you can also give them toys, hiding places, and other sorts of enrichment.

Lifespan

Hedgehog longevity can vary depending on a number of variables, including genetics, food, living conditions, and general health. Hedgehogs can live up to 5-8 years in captivity but only 2–5 years in the wild on average.

A hedgehog kept as a pet can have a long and healthy life with the right care and nourishment. It's crucial to give them a tidy and comfortable place to live, a nutritious diet, and frequent veterinarian treatment. Giving your hedgehog opportunities for physical activity and cerebral stimulation can also assist to advance their general health and wellbeing.

Hedgehogs can be vulnerable to a number of health problems, including obesity, dental disorders, and respiratory infections. Frequent veterinary examinations can help to detect and treat any health issues early on, ensuring that your hedgehog has a longer and better life.

Predators and Threats

In the wild, hedgehogs are threatened by a number of predators, including:

Predators - A variety of animals, including foxes, badgers, owls, domestic cats, and dogs, hunt on hedgehogs. Hedgehogs defend themselves by curling tightly into a ball, leaving just their razor-sharp spines exposed to the predator.

Habitat loss - The survival of hedgehog populations may be at risk due to habitat loss brought on by urbanization, agriculture, and other human activities.

Highway traffic - Hedgehogs frequently get hit by cars when they cross highways, which can result in fatal or serious injuries.

Pesticides and other poisons - Hedgehogs and other wildlife can be harmed by pesticides and other chemicals used in agriculture and gardening.

Climate change – Hedgehogs' food supply and reproductive habits can be impacted by changes in temperature and weather patterns, which can have a detrimental effect on their populations.

Avoid applying pesticides and other chemicals in your garden, provide safe crossing locations for hedgehogs if you live close to a road, and develop habitats for hedgehogs to live in and prosper in to help safeguard hedgehogs and their habitats. Hedgehogs can also be kept alive for future generations by aiding conservation efforts and raising awareness of how critical it is to save them and their habitats.

Legal Issues

Depending on the nation and location, different hedgehog-related legal difficulties arise. Hedgehog ownership may be permitted in some places yet prohibited or requiring a special permit in others.

Hedgehogs cannot be kept as pets in various places in the United States, including California, Hawaii, Georgia, Pennsylvania, and New York City. Hedgehogs may be allowed as pets in several other states, however there may be limitations or rules in place.

Hedgehogs can be kept as pets in the United Kingdom, however it is against the law to release them into the wild. This is due to the possibility that hedgehogs raised in captivity lack the abilities required to live in the wild and may also harbor diseases that could have a negative impact on wild hedgehog populations.

When thinking about getting a hedgehog as a pet, it's crucial to learn the rules and restrictions in your region. Also, it's crucial to ensure that any hedgehog you purchase is from a reputable breeder that has taken the necessary precautions to maintain the animal's health and wellbeing.

Hedgehogs as Pets

If the correct care and attention are given, hedgehogs may be fascinating and satisfying pets. Before introducing a hedgehog into your house, it's crucial to do your homework and make sure it's the correct pet for you.

If you're considering of obtaining a hedgehog as a pet, keep the following in mind:

Housing: Hedgehogs require a spotless, roomy enclosure with lots of space for them to move about and exercise. It is advised to use a cage or enclosure that is at least 4 feet by 2 feet in size.

Diet: Hedgehogs need to eat a variety of protein-rich foods, including insects, lean meat, and premium commercial hedgehog food. Avoid giving children items that are heavy in fat or sugar as this can cause health issues.

Hedgehogs need regular exercise and mental stimulation because they are busy animals. It can be beneficial to keep them entertained and content by giving them toys, places to hide, and chances to explore.

Hedgehogs need frequent veterinary checkups, just like other pets do, to make sure they're healthy and to identify any potential health issues early on.

Hedgehogs can be pleasant and inquisitive creatures, but they are also isolated creatures who may not like to be handled or caressed. It's critical to respect their boundaries and give them lots of chances to play and explore at their own pace.

Ultimately, for those who are prepared to give them the right care and attention, hedgehogs may make fantastic pets. Before bringing one into your home, it's crucial to make sure you can meet their individual demands.

Conclusion

Hedgehogs are intriguing animals with distinctive morphological and behavioral traits. They are well-known for their prickly quills, love of insects, and capacity to curl up into a small ball when threatened. For those who are prepared to give them the right care and attention, hedgehogs may make wonderful pets, but it's crucial to learn about their individual requirements before taking one home.

Hedgehogs in the wild are unfortunately threatened by a variety of factors, such as habitat loss, traffic, and predation. Hedgehogs and their habitats need to be protected, and this can be done by refraining from using pesticides, creating safe places for drivers to cross the road, and supporting conservation initiatives.

Hedgehogs are an unusual and fascinating animal that contribute significantly to many ecosystems. We may contribute to ensuring these beautiful creatures' continued existence by learning more about them.